SMART SLEEP

Just 21 minutes
for deep rest.

Based on
Ancient Science

VIKRAM
ARORA

Smart Sleep

Your New Superpower

2026 Edition

Introducing Smart Sleep (Yoga Nidra)

Vikram Arora

Dedicated to

ShiVi

Introduction

Have you noticed how scoring less sleep has become a weird badge of honor? People actually brag about functioning on 4 or 5 hours.

I've been there before too trying to "power through" work days after pulling all-nighters. But running on fumes just turns you into a zombie, kills creativity, and tanks productivity. It becomes a downward spiral.

Or how about when we sacrifice sleep trying watch "just one more" show on Netflix? Next thing you know, the sun is rising and you're still glued to the TV when you should be sleeping!

We've all experienced the pain of tossing and turning the night before a critical exam, job interview, or big life event. Pre-game jitters feel amplified at 3AM when you're anxious about the future and desperate for rest.

Of course, it is easy to get caught in the web of electronic devices keeping us stimulated late into the night. The blue light from phones and tablets tricks our brains, disrupting natural sleep signals. Before you know it, you've fallen down an Instagram rabbit hole at 2AM when you should be sleeping!

We've all been there… tossing and turning in bed, stressed about tomorrow's big work presentation or final exam, while the clock ticks away precious hours we should be sleeping.

Why is getting quality sleep so elusive in our busy modern lives? What if there was a way to sleep better, wake up feeling refreshed, focused, and ready to conquer the world?

In this book, I'm going to share with you the lost ancient art of scientific sleeping, something I like to call Smart Sleep. It's based on a set of profound relaxation and healing techniques practiced by yogis for thousands of years! I talk about a simplified version of this ancient Indian wisdom, which helps us sleep better and improves our mental health.

Smart Sleeping is different from regular sleeping. It's a special state of deep relaxation for the mind and body that allows you to tap into restorative rest faster. This helps maximize the rejuvenating benefits of sleep so you wake up energized and mentally sharp.

Consider me your personal sleep expert, guiding you up the mountain to better sleep.

With my help, you'll be well-rested and ready to achieve your goals like better physical and mental health, financial freedom, career success, and lasting happiness.

Introduction Part 2: Quality sleep is your superpower

The Global Numbers On Sleep:

The sad truth is despite being more overworked and stressed than ever, we're getting less sleep.

Here are some key statistics:

- Depression affects over 300 million people globally. Sleep problems often accompany depression.

- Insomnia affects 10-30% of adults worldwide. Stress is a major cause of insomnia.

- Approximately 40% of people experience some symptoms of sleep deprivation.

- Irregular sleep patterns and lack of quality sleep affect a huge portion of the workforce due to long or shifting work hours.

This book will share step-by-step techniques to take back control of your sleep and reclaim those lost hours. I'll explain how to create a relaxing pre-sleep routine, calm a busy mind, and wake up feeling refreshed.

The strategies draw from time-tested ancient sleep wisdom infused with my experience and first-hand results.

My goal is to equip you with the knowledge and tools to consistently get restful, high quality sleep, so you can wake up feeling energized and dominate life's challenges. Join me on this journey to unlock your body's true potential through the power of Smart Sleeping!

Chapter List

Prologue

I was working in companies that had night shifts. IBM, Dell, American Express. Good brands, bad life. Mostly night shifts. Started in 2001, went on until 2011. Out of these 10-11 years, there were eight horrific years of working at night and trying to sleep a few hours during the day. Eating food at ungodly hours. Hardly any sleep during the day as well. How can one sleep during the day in metro cities? All of this led to stomach problems, low BP, diabetes, fatigue, lack of appetite.

This also led to my sleep cycle being destroyed. How did i manage to live? I hardly lived after that.

One thing many chronic non-sleepers will relate to, is that after 48 or 72 hours of staying awake, the body and mind refuse to rest even if you lie down on the bed. You are in a state of flight or fight and the body will shake and stand up even if a pin drops. The more we try to sleep, the more the mind gets to know that we are trying to fall asleep. Stressed out about the fact that there hasn't been enough of sleep for so many days, the mind is unable to relax. The caffeine and bad food then starts to do its work.

Many times I resorted to drinking rum or a couple of cans of beer to be able to fall asleep, as advised by friends. Of course that was a temporary solution with further adverse effects.

What did I do? I began looking for ways to get normal again. My sleepless nights were a torture, and I had multiple health issues. I stumbled upon Yoga Nidra, an ancient practice of the Rishis. I learnt it and found it to be useful. I read many books and have been practicing it for over three years.

If I got benefits from Yoga Nidra, then what is this Smart Sleep nonsense?

Yoga Nidra is a deep and profound spiritual practice that helps one attain enlightenment. Now, we don't want deep spirituality and we definitely don't want to leave this world and attain samadhi! We are just mentally and physically tired, and just want some good sleep!

So I striped away the ritualistic, and religious associations/methods from Yoga Nidra and designed a distilled method that is simple and effective in helping us sleep better. We just need to extract the benefit of deep, restful sleep, no matter what we believe in. I know the spiritual benefits too, as the original practice is thousands of years old, but I want everyone to benefit from this, without having a prejudice of the source of knowledge.

Lack of proper sleep is a big problem for millions. This problem paves the way to all kinds of physical, mental and emotional complications. Let's eradicate that.

Most solutions involve dangerous drugs or sleep gadgets that offer no real value. Smart Sleep is the only real, super-easy and holistic solution with zero side-effects.

No gadgets

No chemicals

No devices

No injections

No pills

A way to program your body and mind to access deep rest, anytime.

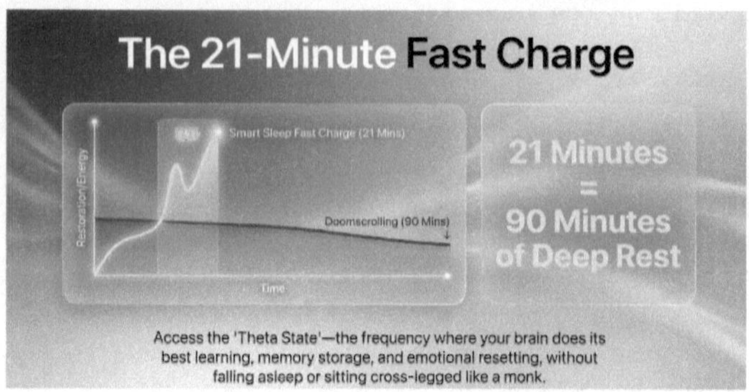

If you require an alarm clock to wake up, you aren't well rested. After you upgrade from accidental sleep to Smart Sleep, you will be deeply rested before morning.

Chapter 1 - You only sleep accidentally

When at night around 1:00 am you finally think of sleeping, you have looked at screens, the giant LED TV, the laptop, the iPad or the iPhone for a good number of hours.

Eyes tired, you try to sleep, with the mind racing. The stuff you saw and read, the reels, the web series, do a slideshow in the mind, each frame lasting a few milliseconds, you get drifted in thoughts, and you keep moving, restless, shaken by the outside noises or phone buzzes.

After a good 30 minutes, you feel like you will now go to sleep, and you do, but accidentally. You don't know the exact minute that you doze off, as you are unconscious.

Sometimes a noise disturbs us at that very crossroad of entering the accidental sleep state and you are stuck again for half an hour.

There is tension as you have set an alarm for 6:30 am and you are worried, that even if you do sleep now, it's only going to be for 4 hours or max 5.

Congratulations, you have again completed your sleep, barely, and accidentally.

Now you wake up and shut off the alarm and doze off. Then you finally awaken after you bad slumber and try to get ready for the day ahead. What a life!

Chapter 2 - Smart Sleep vs accidental Sleep

	Accidental Sleep	Smart Sleep (Yoga Nidra)
Intentionality	Passive, hoping for rest.	Active, precision-engineered protocol.
Nervous System	Easily disrupted by stress hormones.	Guaranteed parasympathetic shift.
Environment	Requires silence, darkness, and a bed.	Works anywhere, even in noisy transit.
Time Investment	7-8 hours (often fragmented).	21 highly concentrated minutes.
Cognitive Output	Baseline survival.	Subconscious reprogramming and peak clarity.

What exactly is smart sleep? And how does it differ from regular shut-eye?

Smart sleeping is based on an ancient deep relaxation technique. It goes by various names, like Yoga Nidra, Non-Sleep Deep Rest (NSDR) and the relaxation response.

Every step of Smart Sleep is scientific.

I call it Smart Sleep because it amplifies the benefits of deep sleep(not the disturbed, accidental sleep we have most of the night) in less time. Think of it like a sleep hack for your mind and body.

Smart Sleep is a redesigned and upgraded version of normal, accidental sleep experienced by most of us.

Why is normal sleep accidental?

You are tired and you succumb to unconscious rest like a log, your body feels better after that.

There is no awareness in your sleep, you drop dead because you are tired.

If you are not tired, or have some problem or worry in your mind, then you are not able to sleep, and you resort to the thing you have available right beside you: Your Smartphone. You scroll Instagram Reels/TikTok/Youtube Shorts, or look at status updates until you drop your phone on your face and finally become unconscious! This, my friends is normal sleep, and it is the worst way to get your shut-eye!

Just because everybody is doing it does not mean it is right!

Digging Deeper

1. Smart Sleep is an active process, not just passive sleeping. You gently guide your awareness through different sensations.

2. It creates a unique state between waking and sleeping. Your brain gets to dip its toes in the restorative waters of sleep even while awake. The ancient yogic technique works here… and one is able to go into theta state while awake.

3. You achieve deeper physical rest faster. Studies show just 21 minutes of Smart Sleep equals about 90 minutes of regular shuteye.

It's my own experience of more than four years I am practicing Smart Sleep.

4. It directly relieves stress and tension. This means you fall asleep faster at night and wake up more refreshed.

5. You access mindfulness, similar to meditation but lying down. I know meditation is impossible for most of us, but Smart Sleep is a natural,

automatic method to get some benefits of the practice, as it allows the busy mind to settle down and recharge.

6. Your body's healing and regulatory systems kick into overdrive, boosting immunity and energy.

Smart sleeping works WITH your normal sleep to enhance its benefits exponentially.

Chapter 3 - Preparing Your Mind and Body for Sleep

Before we get into the specific smart sleep technique, let's set the stage for stellar snoozing. Creating a conducive context will make settling into deep relaxation much easier.

Here are some tips for priming your mind and body:

1. Unplug from devices - Blue light from screens delays the release of melatonin, the key sleep hormone. Avoid digital stimulation for 1-2 hours before going into Smart Sleep.

2. Get comfy - Wear loose pajamas that don't bind. Have an extra blanket nearby in case you get chilly. Use pillows to support limbs and align your spine.

3. Set the mood - Dim lights, play white noise, adjust the temperature, create total darkness and silence. Make your sleeping cave comfortable.

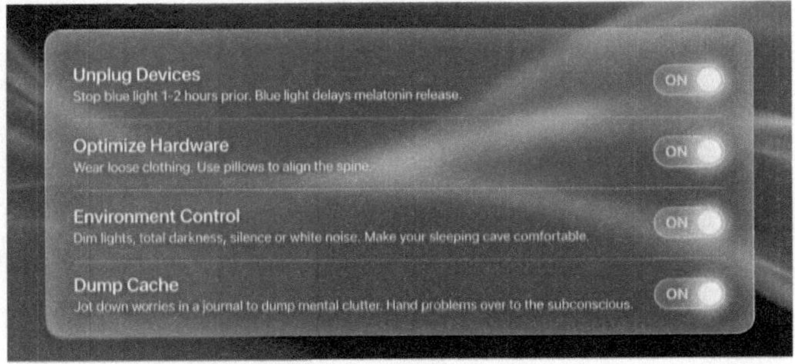

4. Let go of the day - Jot worries in a journal to dump mental clutter. Visualize handing problems to your subconscious to solve overnight.

The goal is to set up the ideal restful vibes from both a mental and physical perspective. Your sleep environment contributes bigly to quality of rest.

Tuning your body through intention and senses is half the battle.

Chapter 4 - Mastering the Smart Sleep Technique: The Four Steps

Now, I'll walk you through the four step formula.

Find a quiet place where you can lie down without distraction. Situate any props to make you ultra comfy.

STEP ONE: Taking Deep Breaths

Lying on your back, close your eyes and start taking slow, full breaths. Feel your chest and belly rise as you inhale, and fall as you exhale.

Focussing on your breath while you inhale and exhale isn't easy for even this much time, as there will be flashes of thoughts cluttering up your brain, along with itches and discomfort in various parts of the body. You can move a little if the need arises, but try to relax! This initial settling down is the most challenging part of the entire technique, because most of us cannot sit still.

Time Duration: 2 to 3 minutes.

STEP TWO: Solving the noise problem with **Sound-Scan**

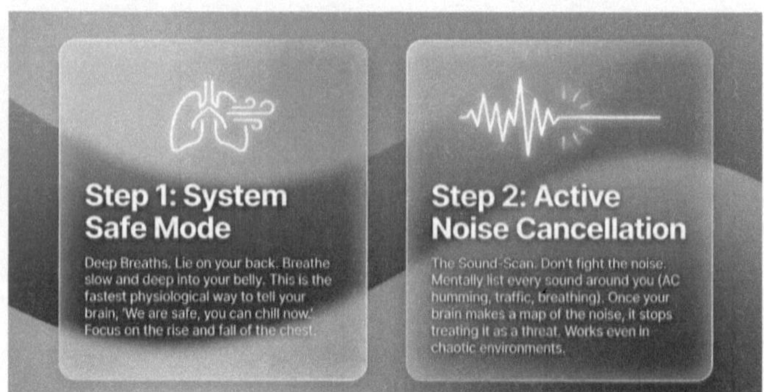

There is an ancient science behind Smart Sleep, and it takes care of the noise issue in the smartest way possible!

Just scan and take a mental note of all the noises/sounds around you, the dog barking outside, the noise in the kitchen, the car speeding outside, the air conditioner humming, and even the noise of your own breath. Once the mind does a 'sound scan' of the surroundings, you will be able to perform Smart Sleep even with all the commotion! The mind makes a map of all the sounds coming, and will now get in deep sleep more regardless of those sounds, provided they are not too loud in the beginning.

Once you are an expert, you can complete a Smart Sleep 21-minute programming even if there is a war going on outside. I am not making this up! Napoleon, the emperor of France did the same in the 17th century! It is documented in many places.

Time Duration: 1 minute

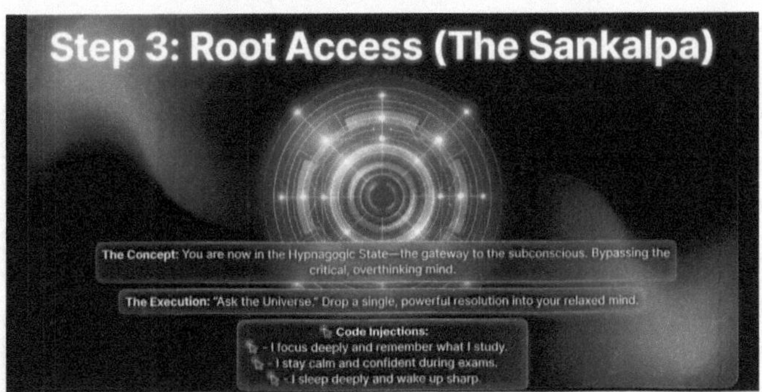

STEP THREE: Ask The Universe

You become aware of your relaxing body along with the series of thoughts coming into your mind, and **ask the Universe** for a restful break which will rejuvenate you.

Now I know the thoughts can't stop, but you simply let them come and make the request to the Universe to help you out for just a few minutes while you complete the main step coming next.

Time Duration: Less than 1 minute

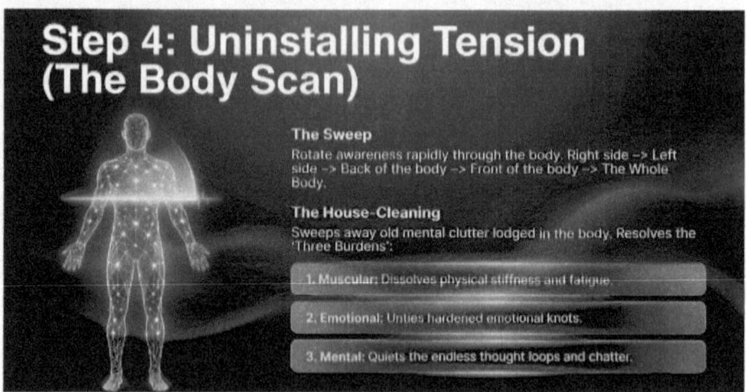

STEP FOUR: The Body Scan

Begin to relax your body completely, starting with your toes and working your way up to your head.

As you bring your awareness to each part of your body, repeat the following affirmations to yourself while focusing on the specific body part, beginning with the frontal body:

Now, begin the body scan.

Let your mind mentally feel your body parts, beginning with the right hand:

Right thumb, index finger, middle finger, ring finger, little finger, palm of your hand, back of your hand, wrist, forearm, elbow, upper arm, shoulder, armpit, side, waist, hip, thigh, knee, lower leg, ankle, heel, front of the foot, sole of the foot, all the right toes.

Continue on the left side:

Bring your attention to the left hand, left thumb, index finger, middle finger, ring finger, little finger, palm of your hand, back of the hand, wrist, forearm, elbow, upper arm, shoulder, armpit, side, waist, hip, thigh, knee, lower leg, ankle, heel, front of the foot, sole of the foot, all the left toes.

Let your attention move to the back of your body:

Start with the heels resting on the floor, calves, backs of the knees, backs of the thighs, buttocks, lower back, middle back, upper back, back of the arms, backs of the hands, shoulders, back of the neck, back of the head, crown of your head, both the ears, forehead, eyebrows, eyebrow center, eyes, nose, tip of the nose, cheeks, jaw, lips, chin, front of the neck, collarbones, fronts of the arms and hands. Return to your chest, continue with your solar plexus, upper abdomen, lower abdomen, inner organs, fronts of the hips, fronts of the thighs, fronts of the knees. Lower legs, ankles, fronts of the feet. All the toes.

Now mentally feel your whole body all at once.

Once you have brought your awareness to your whole body, focus on your breath again.

Continue to observe your breath for as long as you like.

You can repeat the body scan two to three times, as it is a crucial step.

Try and recall what you had asked the universe in step three.

Time Duration: 15 minutes

Notes on Step Four:

Imagine your breath flowing as relaxing light to different body parts. This peaceful visualization enhances relaxation.

After completing the full body scan, keep breathing steadily while maintaining light awareness. If thoughts arise, gently return focus to your overall sense of stillness. Keep things slow. Slowing down makes you live your life for a few minutes. Otherwise we are just completing one task after another.

When you are through, gently stretch your body before opening your eyes and resuming activity.

That's the basic Smart Sleep technique.

With practice, you'll learn to enter even deeper states of smart sleep for amplified benefits.

21 Minutes of Smart Sleep equals 90 minutes of deep rest.

Chapter 5 - What Smart Sleep feels like

Action: Progressive rotation of consciousness from toes to head, visualizing breath as healing energy.

The Mechanism: Systematically releases stored muscular and nervous system tension.

Advanced Layers: Integrating opposite sensations (heaviness vs. lightness) accelerates physical recovery and forces the mind to remain highly focused, preventing accidental sleep.

Initially, it's slightly discomforting, as there are a lot of old thoughts, really old thoughts, stuck inside your joints and muscles giving you stress, aches and pains(as stupid as it sounds).

When i started doing this practice, the body scan part left me stranded at a particular body part, like the knee or the elbow, and a certain thought something that was bothering me unconsciously for years/decades and had nested itself inside my body suddenly comes back to surface, in my mind and i am surprised at what am i thinking out of the blue?

I ask myself how the hell is this possible that this thought/memory, which is so old, like me being scolded by my dad when i was 9, or me travelling to a watery place with cousins when i was 12, suddenly surface itself? and why?

I began to realize that the smart sleep/yoga nidra is doing some initial house-cleaning, and sweeping away old mental clutter, now lodged in the body.

Like when you sweep a house after years, there is a lot of stuff, dirt, old papers, toys, etc you find that you never knew you would, or it had not been in your living memory any more, so you are surprised to find it. The body is too was working like a clunky old attic that you now are cleaning at a cellular level.

After a few weeks, you witness yourself dozing off, going in a trance, with a mild snore that clears your mind like a motor. When you finally complete the practice session after 20 to 30 minutes, you look at the clock and you have no idea about the time. You are surprised that it's only been 30 minutes.

In your mind, you are so well rested it could easily have been two hours, if you were doing normal sleep.

Dozing off while doing smart sleep is fine. It just means your body is self-optimizing for rest, and decided it needs to heal on a basic level first.

Chapter 6 - What all Smart Sleep does?

The Antifragile Executive Ecosystem

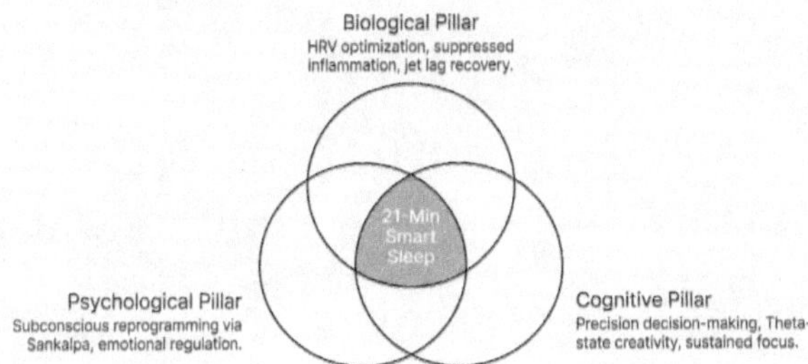

Smart Sleep is a full-body reset that taps into your natural healing power. The science is real, and the perks are wild.

Check this out:

- Drops Inflammation: Deep rest cuts the stuff that causes pain and ages you—fewer aches, fewer sick days.

- Fixes Hormones: Stress and sleep vibes balance out, boosting mood, energy, and immunity.

- Lowers Blood Pressure: Relaxation flips your chill switch, easing the strain.

- Sharpens Your Brain: Neurons fire better—focus, memory, smarts all level up.

- Slows Aging: It flips on anti-aging genes, keeping you young inside.

- Fights Cancer: Rest powers up your immune system's cancer-killing crew.

- Lifts Your Mind: Anxiety and depression? It's a natural, no-side-effect fix.

It's like hitting refresh on your whole system, clearing out stress gunk—physical, mental, emotional.

Chapter 7- The Sleeping Pill

This is from a 2008 blog post of mine:

A sizable population of our world takes sleeping pills regularly. I am often amazed at this assumption that people take while consuming the sleeping pill.

They think this pill is going to make them sleep. Nothing could be farther from the truth.

Just how wrong these huge number of sleeping pill poppers are... that pill does not make them sleep, instead it's a forceful and brutal cutoff of the brain and the body forcing them to faint and be unconscious. They intentionally make themselves pass out. They don't wake up refreshed, they wake up as if someone hit them hard with a bat on the head and they passed out for a few hours. They didn't dream anything, they were in a mild coma! These people in most cases know all this, but their lives are so complicated and messed up they take the pill as an escape for a few hours, they konk themselves out for some time so that they feel they have rested.

It is common knowledge that taking a large dose of this pill is a form of suicide. If taking 10 of them can kill you right away, then isn't taking 1 killing you a little too?

Smells like machines!

Pill poppers want instant results. They want Extra Strength painkillers, super strong aspirins, Super fast 'sleeping' pills.... they want these results at the cost of their health. Make them sleep, fast....don't they know they already are in such a slumber sleep such a unaware state, they want to slide down further....

Gladly! Get your doses and pop those pills lets drown your sorrows, your pains, lets melt your mind, fuck with your stomach, your liver, your brain, your blood, your heart, let it clot, let it stop, don't stop those pills, brother.

Chapter 8 - The Art of Systematic Relaxation

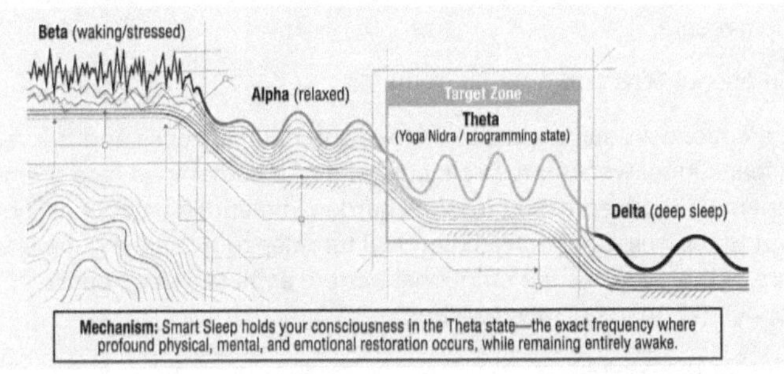

Mechanism: Smart Sleep holds your consciousness in the Theta state—the exact frequency where profound physical, mental, and emotional restoration occurs, while remaining entirely awake.

Lets do a short recap of everything:

The foundation of Smart Sleep comes from an ancient yogic practice known as placing awareness—directing the mind with precision to different parts of the body. Over time, I refined and simplified this age-old method into a modern, accessible system that anyone can practice, regardless of background or belief.

The essence of this method is simple: train the mind to relax the body consciously and release layers of tension from within. Modern life constantly feeds tension into our system. Whether it's overthinking, physical inactivity, or emotional strain, the body and mind collect stress like static electricity. Left unchecked, these tensions accumulate into three major burdens—muscular, emotional, and mental.

Conquering Life's Three Burdens

1. Muscular Tensions

These tensions are tied to our physical body and nervous system. They show up as stiffness, fatigue, or restlessness. Through Smart Sleep, the body is guided into deep physical relaxation, dissolving these tensions layer by layer. Muscles loosen, the breath slows, and the entire nervous system resets.

2. Emotional Tensions

Our emotions are full of dualities—love and hate, success and failure, joy and fear. Often, we suppress difficult emotions rather than face them. Over time, these repressed feelings harden into subtle emotional knots. Smart Sleep helps quiet this emotional turbulence by calming the deeper layers of the mind. As the emotional system settles, a deep sense of balance and peace begins to emerge.

3. Mental Tensions

The mind, when overactive, becomes its own source of stress. Endless thought loops, confusion, and inner chatter exhaust our mental energy. Smart Sleep allows the mind to rest consciously, leading awareness into the quieter dimensions beneath the surface of thought. In this stillness, clarity and inner silence naturally arise.

Ordinary sleep often leaves these tensions unresolved. The body may rest, but the mind continues its restless activity. Smart Sleep is different— it's a process of conscious rest. One hour of practice can equal several hours of normal sleep in terms of restfulness and recovery. It's a scientific method to recharge both body and mind.

The real strength of Smart Sleep lies in what happens when the body rests and the mind stays quietly awake. During practice, awareness enters a state between wakefulness and sleep. Psychologists call this the hypnagogic state—a gateway to the subconscious mind.

In this state, we introduce a short, clear, and positive statement known as a Resolution. It might be something like, "I am calm and confident," or "I am healing every day." Unlike ordinary affirmations, a Resolution made during Smart Sleep goes straight into the subconscious, bypassing the critical mind. It takes root deeply and begins to shape behavior and attitude from within.

A Resolution created in this state doesn't just satisfy surface desires. It restructures one's life pattern—physically, mentally, emotionally, and even spiritually.

Smart Sleep is, in essence, a science of conscious withdrawal from the senses. When awareness is intentionally guided away from the external world and physical body, what remains is pure consciousness—alert, calm, and immensely powerful.

A core technique in the practice is the rotation of awareness. Here, the mind is guided to move rapidly through different points of the body— head, shoulders, chest, arms, legs, and so on. This rotation clears neural pathways, synchronizes the body's internal systems, and deeply relaxes the mind.

As the practice deepens, you move through layers of your own personality—from the outer physical layer to the subtle mental one, and finally to the space where thought ceases entirely. This inner stillness is not empty; it's the source of creativity and insight.

Many breakthroughs in science and art have arisen from such states of relaxed awareness—when Kekulé dreamed of the circular structure of benzene or when Einstein visualized time and space merging.

In Smart Sleep, the goal is not to drift into unconscious sleep but to remain gently aware as the body rests. Even brief moments of awareness in this state are powerful enough to plant seeds of transformation in the subconscious.

Smart Sleep is a training in conscious living. Regular practice transforms an individual burdened by stress into one who is centered, calm, and internally strong. You begin to notice better focus, improved memory, emotional stability, and deeper intuition.

This practice offers more than relief from tension. It awakens a new way of experiencing rest and awareness—where sleep becomes a tool for self-evolution rather than escape.

Smart Sleep teaches you to rest consciously, to release completely, and to awaken fully—refreshed, creative, and free.

About me:

I am a writer and trainer, practicing yoga nidra for over six years now. I am on social media as @neoviky

www.ingramcontent.com/pod-product-compliance
Lightning Source LLC
Chambersburg PA
CBHW021139260726
48656CB00023B/973